Farmers! Planting, Nurturing and Harvesting

Farming for Kids

Children's Agriculture Books

BABY PROFESSOR

EDUCATION KIDS

Farmers are the people who plant, cultivate and harvest the fruits, vegetales and even the meat you love to eat.

Planting

Planting crops is one of the things a farmer does.

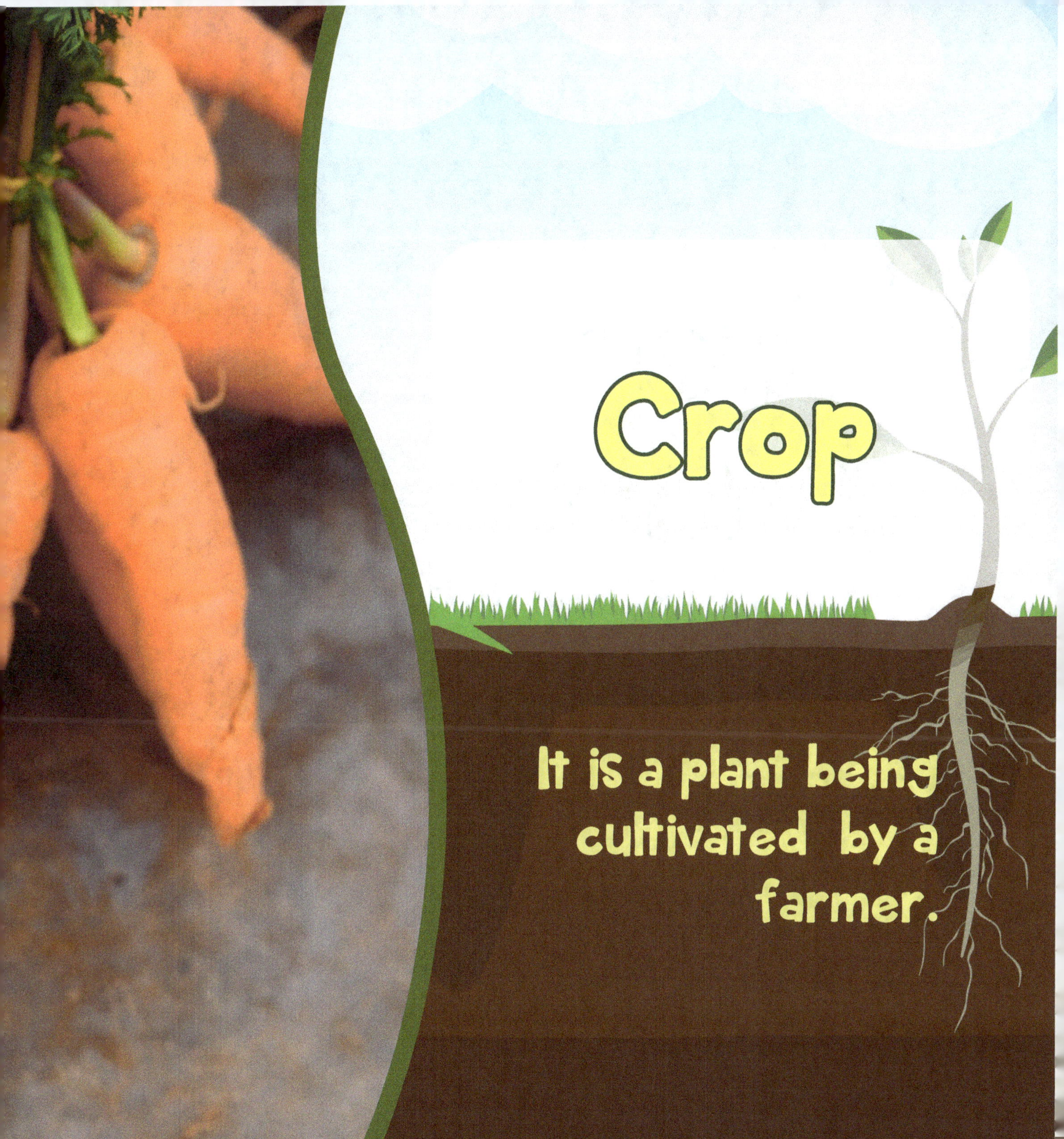

Crop
It is a plant being cultivated by a farmer.

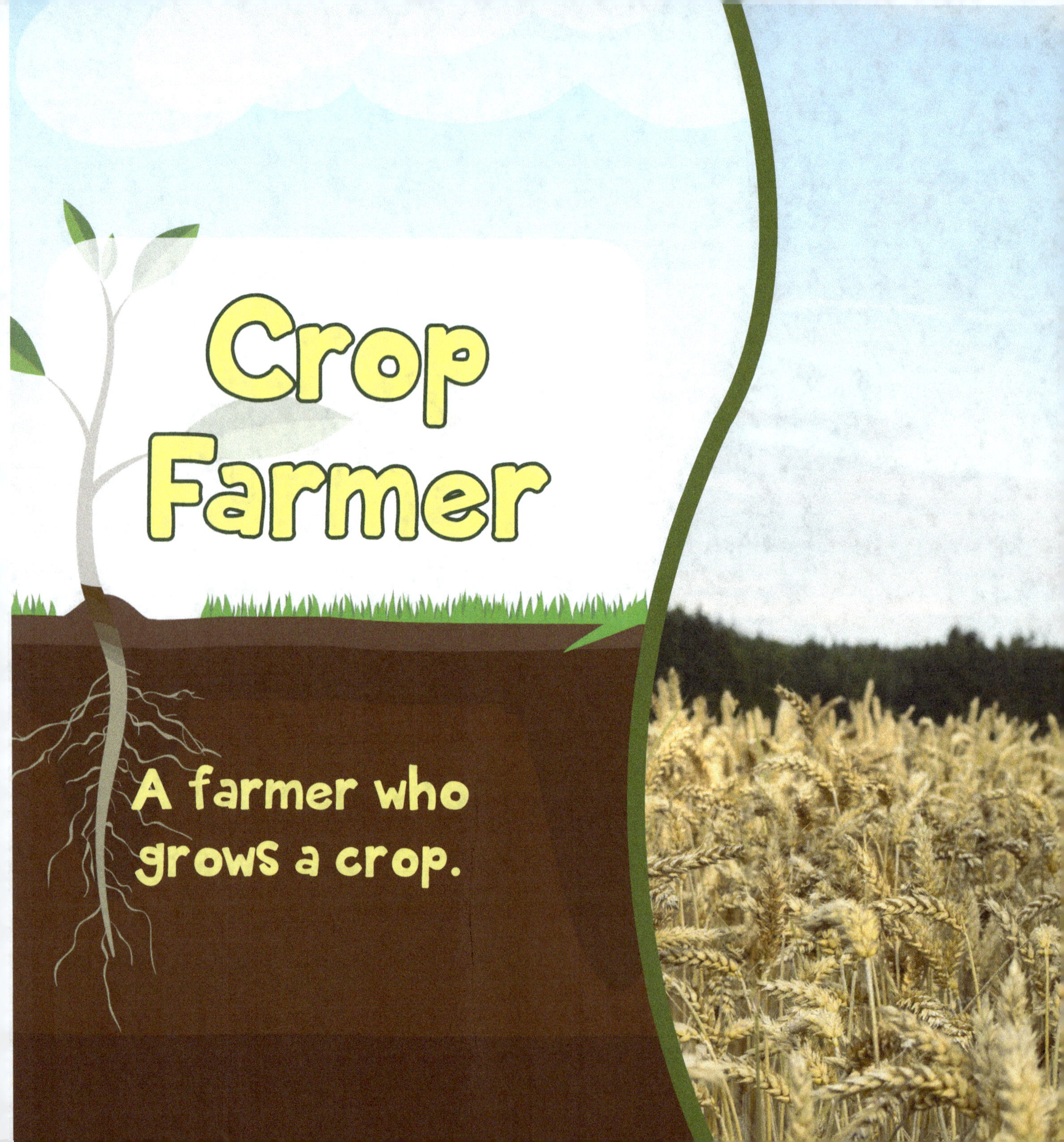
Crop
Farmer
A farmer who
grows a crop.

FRESH
LOCAL
PRODUCE

Common Crops

The common crops are Carrots, potatoes and any vegetables and fruits we eat.

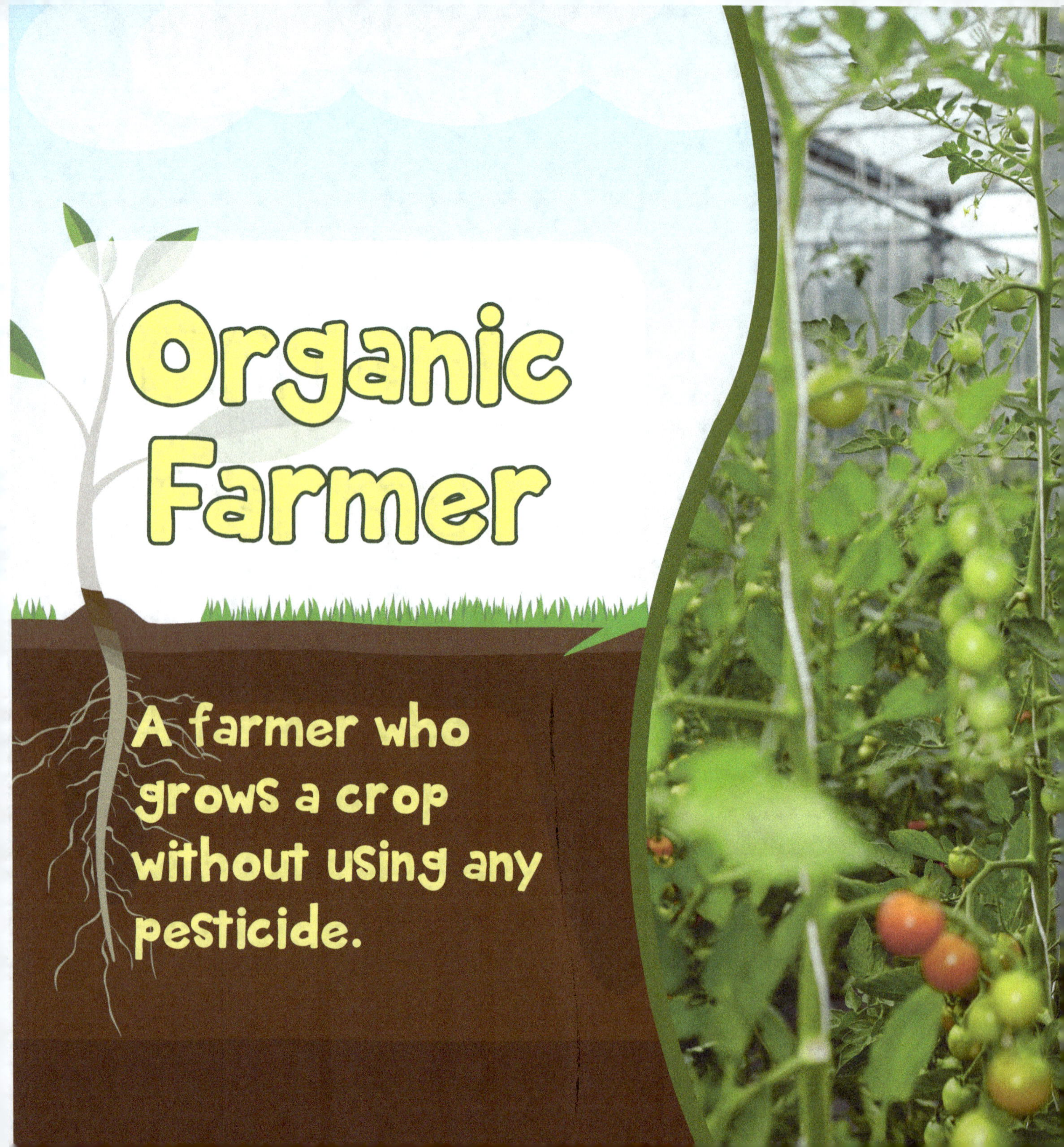

Organic Farmer
A farmer who grows a crop without using any pesticide.

Nurturing
A farmer nurtures the crops to make sure it grows healthy.

The photo shows
a plant being
nurtured by a
farmer.

Quality Crops

Farmers make sure that the crops are growing well to produce a good quality crop.

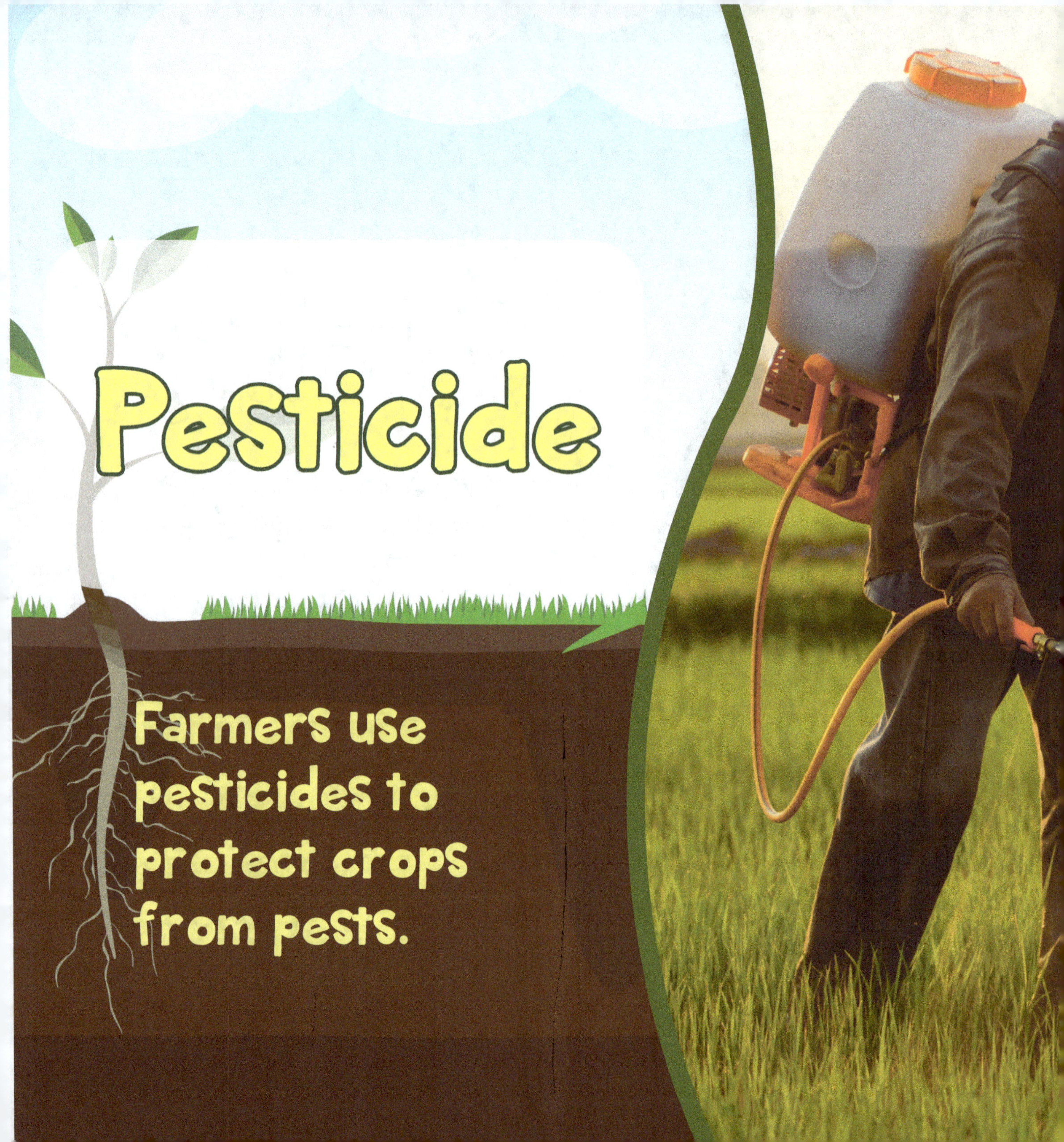
Pesticide
Farmers use pesticides to protect crops from pests.

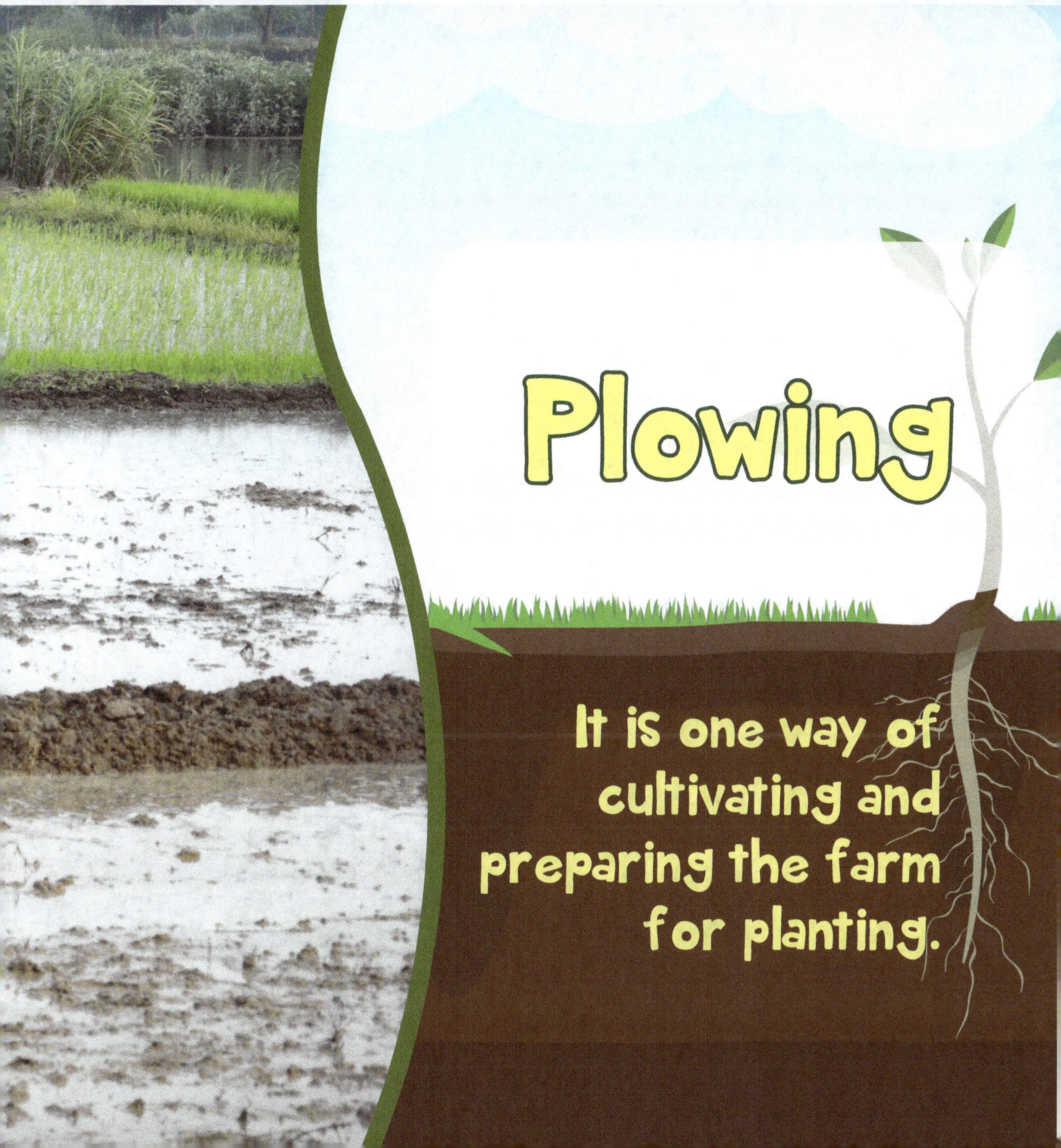

Plowing

It is one way of
cultivating and
preparing the farm
for planting.

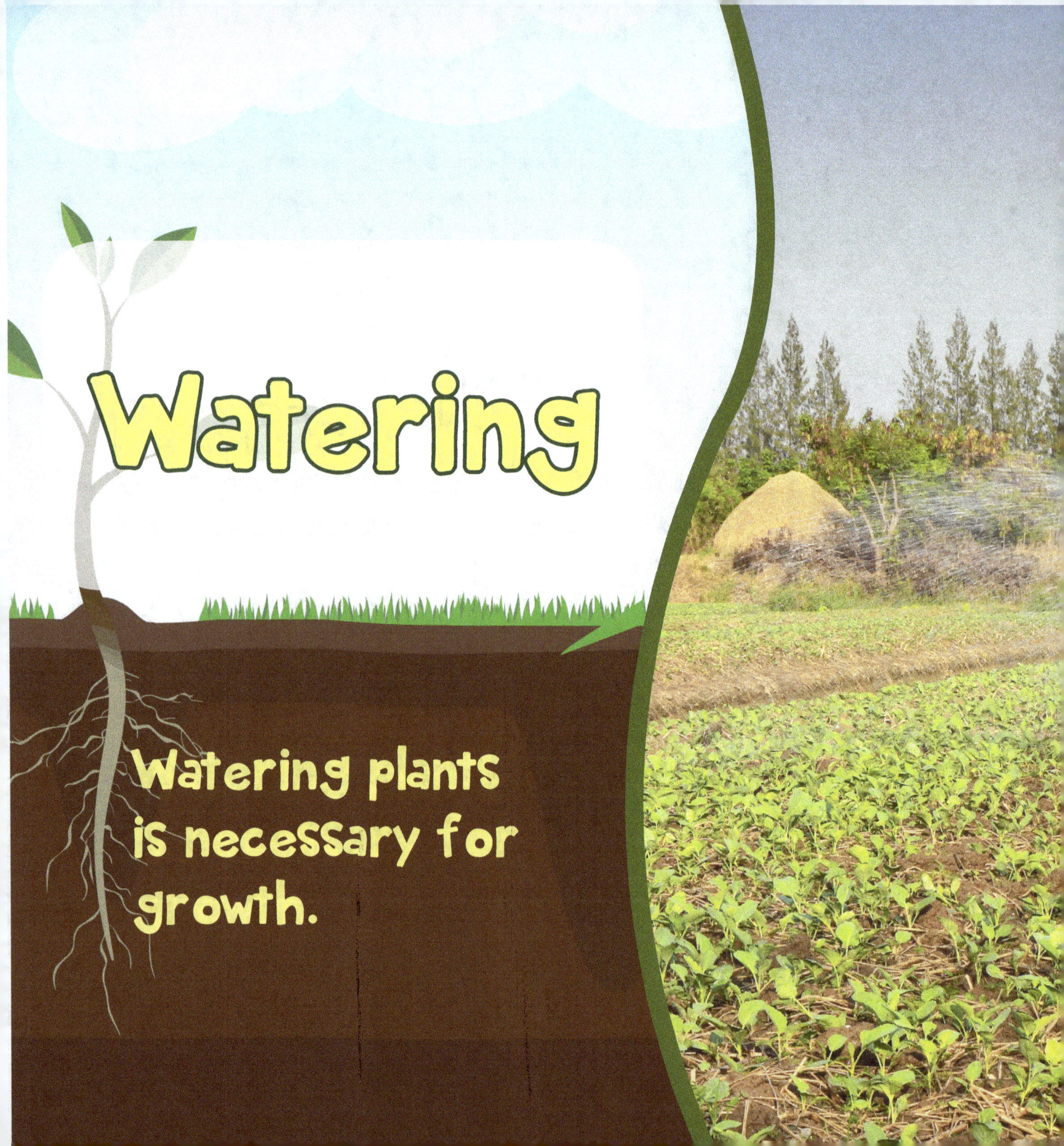

Watering

Watering plants is necessary for growth.

Weeds
These are the
unwanted plants.

The farmer in the
photo is watering
the vineyard
using a modern
equipment.

Farm
A photo of a nurtured and well cultivated farm.

Screens

Screens all over
the crops to
avoid pests.

Harvest
The carrots are ready for harvest.

Organic vegetables
The harvest of the organic vegetables.

Do you Find Farmers Great?

Make your own garden and apply what you read from this book.

Enjoy doing
Great!

Visit
BABY PROFESSOR
EDUCATION KIDS
www.BabyProfessorBooks.com
to download Free Baby Professor eBooks
and view our catalog of new and exciting
Children's Books